WITHDRAWN

WITHDRAWN

Easter

by Mari C. Schuh

Consulting Editor: Gail Saunders-Smith, Ph.D.

Consultant: Alexa Sandmann, Ed.D.
Professor of Literacy
The University of Toledo
Member, National Council for the Social Studies

Pebble Books

an imprint of Capstone Press
Mankato, Minnesota

Pebble Books are published by Capstone Press
151 Good Counsel Drive, P.O. Box 669, Mankato, Minnesota 56002
http://www.capstone-press.com

Copyright © 2003 Capstone Press. All rights reserved.
No part of this publication may be reproduced in whole or in part, or stored in a
retrieval system, or transmitted in any form or by any means, electronic, mechanical,
photocopying, recording, or otherwise, without written permission of the publisher.
For information regarding permission, write to Capstone Press,
151 Good Counsel Drive, P.O. Box 669, Dept. R, Mankato, Minnesota 56002.
Printed in the United States of America.

1 2 3 4 5 6 07 06 05 04 03 02

Library of Congress Cataloging-in-Publication Data
Schuh, Mari C., 1975–
    Easter / by Mari C. Schuh.
    p. cm.—(Holidays and celebrations)
    Summary: Simple text and photographs describe the history of Easter and
the many ways in which it is celebrated.
    Includes bibliographical references and index.
    ISBN 0-7368-1445-0 (hardcover)
    ISBN 0-7368-9398-9 (paperback)
    1. Easter—Juvenile literature. [1. Easter. 2. Holidays.] I. Title. II. Series.
GT4935 .S345 2003
394.2667—dc21   2001008486

Note to Parents and Teachers

The Holidays and Celebrations series supports national social
studies standards related to culture. This book describes Easter
and illustrates how it is celebrated. The photographs support early
readers in understanding the text. The repetition of words and
phrases helps early readers learn new words. This book also
introduces early readers to subject-specific vocabulary words, which
are defined in the Words to Know section. Early readers may need
assistance to read some words and to use the Table of Contents,
Words to Know, Read More, Internet Sites, and Index/Word List
sections of the book.

Table of Contents

4

Easter is a spring holiday.
People celebrate Easter
on a Sunday in March
or April.

6

Christians celebrate Easter
in church. They honor
a man named Jesus.
Christians believe that
Jesus went up to heaven.

Christians go to church on Easter. They celebrate the life of Jesus. Many churches are decorated with Easter lilies.

Some families eat special meals together on Easter. They might eat ham or lamb.

rabbit

daffodils

lambs

chicks

12

Easter is a time
to celebrate new life
in spring.

People color eggs
on Easter. They dye
them many colors.

Children wait for the Easter Bunny to visit. They hope he will bring them baskets filled with treats.

Some children have Easter egg hunts. They look for hidden eggs and candy.

Life begins again
in spring. Easter
celebrates new life.

Words to Know

celebrate—to do something fun on a special day

Christian—a person who believes in Jesus

Easter Bunny—a make-believe bunny that is popular during Easter; the Easter Bunny is believed to give candy and eggs to children on Easter.

Easter lily—a tall plant with big, white flowers; Easter lily flowers are shaped like a trumpet.

holiday—a special day that people celebrate

Jesus—the main teacher of a religion called Christianity; Christians believe that Jesus is the son of God.

Read More

Harrast, Tracy L. *The Easter Story.* Peek-a-Bible. Grand Rapids, Mich.: Zonderkidz, 2000.

Marx, David F. *Easter.* Rookie Read-about Holidays. New York: Children's Press, 2001.

Merrick, Patrick. *Easter Bunnies.* Holiday Symbols. Chanhassen, Minn.: Child's World, 2000.

Winne, Joanne. *Let's Get Ready for Easter.* Celebrations. New York: Children's Press, 2001.

Internet Sites

Easter and Spring Crafts and Activities
http://www.EnchantedLearning.com/crafts/easter

Easter for Kids and Teachers
http://www.kiddyhouse.com/holidays/easter

Kids Domain—Bunny Ears for Kids
http://kidsdomain.com/craft/bunnyears.html

Index/Word List

April, 5
believe, 7
celebrate, 5, 7,
  9, 13, 21
children, 17, 19
Christians, 7, 9
church, 7, 9
color, 15
decorated, 9
dye, 15

Easter Bunny, 17
eat, 11
egg, 15, 19
families, 11
heaven, 7
holiday, 5
honor, 7
hope, 17
hunts, 19
Jesus, 7, 9

life, 9,
  13, 21
lilies, 9
March, 5
meals, 11
new, 13, 21
people, 5, 15
spring, 5, 13, 21
Sunday, 5
treats, 17

Word Count: 127
Early-Intervention Level: 14

Credits

Heather Kindseth, series designer; Patrick D. Dentinger, book designer;
  Wanda Winch, photo researcher; Nancy White, photo stylist

Capstone Press/Gary Sundermeyer, cover, 1
Folio Inc./Fred Maroon, 12 (upper right); David Harp, (lower left)
International Stock/George Ancona, 14; Bill Stanton, 10
Photri-Microstock/Lani Novak Howe, 16
Susanne Thornburg, 12 (upper left)
TimePix/Mansell, 6
Unicorn Stock Photos/Ed Harp, 18; Martha McBride, 8 (inset), 20
USDA/ARS/Keith Weller, 12 (lower right)
Visuals Unlimited/Jeff Greenberg, 8
Xi Lien, 4

The author dedicates this book to her rabbit, Karma.